screen
printing

OTHER ARTS & CRAFTS BOOKS

Batik as a Hobby
Prints—from Linoblocks and Woodcuts
Coloring Papers
Composition in Art
Creative Paper Crafts in Color
Designs—and How to Use Them
How to Attract Attention with Your Art
Modern Geometric Design
Postercraft
Potato Printing
Practical Encyclopedia of Crafts
Scene Design

screen
printing

By HEINRICH BIRKNER

STERLING
PUBLISHING CO., INC. NEW YORK

Oak Tree Press Co., Ltd.
London & Sydney

Credits for completed screen prints:

page 6	"Still Life with Fruit in Gray" by Burghild Keller
page 7	Pupil's work
page 8	"Women in Rhodes" by Angelika Eisbein
page 9	Pupil's work
pages 66 and 67	Author's work
page 70	"White Flowers" by Ilsegard Reiner; "Lace Pigeon" by Burghild Keller
page 71	"Flower Fragments" by Manfred Henniger
page 74	"Red Symbol" by Professor Eichberger
page 75	"Fruits" by Ilsegard Reiner; "Chickens" by Wiltraud Jaspers
page 78	"Penguins" by Wiltraud Jaspers
page 79	Print made from a pastel drawing by Ida Kerkovius
page 86	"Shore with Reeds"
page 90	Christmas picture by Wiltraud Jaspers
page 91	"Horses and Riders" by Roland Dorfler; "Maya Art" poster

Translated by Kenneth T. Dutfield
Adapted by Jane Lassner

Originally published under the title "Siebdruck" by
Otto Maier Verlag, © 1968, Ravensburg, Germany

Second Printing, 1972
Copyright © 1971 by Sterling Publishing Co., Inc.
419 Park Avenue South, New York, N.Y. 10016
British edition published by Oak Tree Press Co., Ltd., Nassau, Bahamas
Distributed in Australia by Oak Tree Press Co., Ltd.,
P.O. Box 34, Brickfield Hill, Sydney 2000, N.S.W.
Distributed in the United Kingdom and elsewhere in the British Commonwealth
by Ward Lock Ltd., 116 Baker Street, London W 1
Manufactured in the United States of America
All rights reserved
Library of Congress Catalog Card No.: 79-151713
ISBN 0-8069- 5170-2   UK 7061 2302 6
5171-0

CONTENTS

Illus. 1. Fuzzy outlines add to the abstract nature of "Still Life with Fruit in Gray" by Burghild Keller. For a picture with varying shades of one color, you might treat the different shades as separate colors, making different stencils for each one. Or, make only one stencil with varying degrees of opacity in different sections, to block out differing amounts of ink.

1. THE PRINCIPLES OF SCREEN PRINTING

Screen printing, also called "silk screen printing" or "serigraphy," was once confined to the professional art world and the poster-making trade. Because of the recent invention of special inks and other screen printing aids, even amateur artists and craftsmen are taking advantage of this inexpensive method of printing a small number of posters or of decorating fabric and other materials. Screen printing demands patience, a careful hand, and an eye for artistic effects. If you have these, you are well on your way to making good screen prints, for the process is not difficult, though it can be time-consuming.

The basic principle of screen printing is simple to understand: imagine a series of finely meshed screens of fabric stretched tightly over wooden frames. You either paint stencils on the screens with a special liquid, or cut them from stencil paper and attach them to the screens with an adhesive. Ink is rapidly forced through the screen with a rubber squeegee, similar to the implement which a window washer uses, to color both the screen and the printing surface beneath the screen. The stencils block the ink from coming through certain places on the screen, leaving portions of the printing surface free of ink. The pattern which is printed in the screen process is what you have stencilled as a design.

The elements of the screen printing process were probably first used by the ancient Chinese and Egyptians, while Europeans did not know of the craft until the end of the 19th century. Once the basic principles became known in the Western world, the

Illus. 2. In screen printing, soft areas of shading as well as solid areas with sharp edges are possible. "Child's Head" shows both techniques.

popularity of the process spread rapidly: sign painters and fabric decorators were enthusiastic about the process, and quick-drying inks and other aids were quickly invented. While there are now mechanically operated screen presses which can make several thousand prints an hour, the original hand-operated equipment can never be completely replaced: the hand operation allows printing on *any* material, in *any* size, and a machine does not. The subtle differences which are inevitable among the individual prints in a series make each one a work of art, valued because of its uniqueness. Screen prints by famous artists are quite expensive to buy and, usually, quite beautiful.

ADVANTAGES OF SCREEN PRINTING

Everyone who makes screen prints is enthusiastic about the unusual characteristics and advantages of this technique. Because of the low cost of the basic materials, screen printing allows even a small number of posters, signs, illustrations, placards, place mats, wall hangings, etc., to be produced economically. Vast mechanical preparations, which might be worth the effort for large quantities, are not necessary here. Unlike other methods of reproduction in several colors, multicolor screen printing is no more complex or expensive than printing in one

Illus. 3. A photographic stencil formed the thin lines and details of the faces of this screen print, called "Women in Rhodes." Photographic stencils require a lot of equipment and experience, but you will be able to achieve a similar effect by using the less complex stencils described later.

color, although it does call for exact register or placement of the stencils. Also, in screen printing the print is the same as the original, and not its mirror-image. This feature is especially welcomed by amateurs.

The equipment for screen printing can be bought already assembled, or made from scratch for considerably less money by almost anyone. Screen printing can be safely done without any previous knowledge or experience with other printing processes, and is an excellent medium to teach in schools.

The visual effects obtained from screen printing are almost unlimited. You can make screen prints with sharp outlines and fine lines, simulating linoleum or wood block prints and pen-and-ink drawings. Or, by using shellacs and other liquid adhesives which are painted on the screen and then partially dissolved, you can produce a grained effect similar to a lithograph, with shading and soft edges around the areas of color. Even more versatility is possible because of the large number of materials on which screen prints can be made: paper and fabric are the most common, but with the proper inks, it is possible to print on wood, glass, leather, metal, plastic, and even foam rubber.

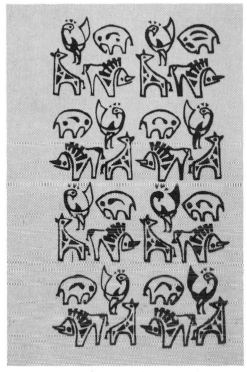

Illus. 4. Decorative animal motifs are suitable for printing a "repeat" design on cloth. You lift and move the screen to a second place, and then make a new print.

2. A SAMPLE PROJECT

Before you invest a lot of time, money and energy into buying and building your screen printing equipment, why not build a mock-up of a frame and squeegee by using ordinary materials from around your home? The print you obtain with this equipment will not be of very good quality, but the purpose of this experiment is not to produce a perfect print. Rather, it will make you aware of the techniques of screen printing, as well as the limitations of the process.

Make your frame from strips of cardboard (shirtboard thickness). Cut 6 strips of 8½″ length, and 6 strips of 6½″ length, all about 1″ wide. Glue 3 strips of the same length on their flat side to each other so the strip is

3 layers thick. Make 4 such layered strips. Tape the layered strips together to form a rectangular frame (see illustration). Use masking tape or cellophane tape at the corners, and cover the corners completely so the paint cannot ooze into the joints.

For the screen, use an old nylon or silk stocking. Naturally the gauge—the closeness of the weave of the threads—will not be a very tight one, and you will not be able to obtain too much accuracy or fine line detail in your print. For experimental purposes, however, the stocking is satisfactory. Cut a rectangle from the stocking the same dimensions as the outer size of the cardboard frame, plus at least 1″ on each side. Place the nylon

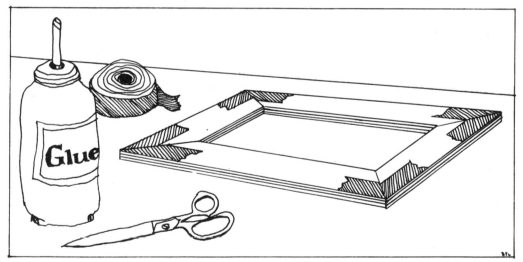

Illus. 5. For your sample project, construct a frame of cardboard strips. Each side of the rectangle should be three layers thick, with glue between the layers to hold the pieces together. The corners should be mitered, and then securely taped together.

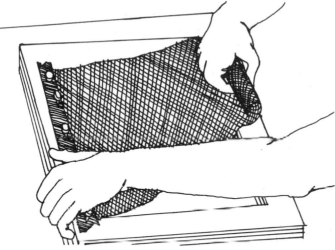

Illus. 6. Cut an old stocking so you have a rectangular piece large enough to cover the cardboard frame. Attach the stocking along one side of the frame with thumbtacks; then stretch the stocking taut and tack it to the opposite side. To prevent the stocking from tearing, put tape between the stocking and the tacks.

rectangle flat on the table, and center the cardboard frame on top of it. Fold the margins of the stocking up along the sides of the frame and, using the same tape you used to seal the corners of the frame, tape the screen to the cardboard. Make sure the stocking is stretched across the frame as tightly as your materials will permit. The tape prevents the stocking from running. Now tack a series of thumbtacks into the frame to hold the silk securely. (See drawing.)

Next cover 1½" width along the short sides of the screen with masking tape. When you later place the paint dabs on to the screen, place it in one of these areas. The paint will not go through the screen along the borders, so the edges of your print will be sharp and the corners square.

Use an ordinary wax crayon—of any shade—as the block-out material for the stencil. With the nylon side flat on the table, and a sheet of newspaper underneath the screen (so you do not crayon on the table), draw a design on the open area of the screen. You can draw on either side of the screen, but if you draw letters, remember to draw their mirror-image if you are going to turn the screen over for printing. Do not make the design too fussy: a simple solid shape or two and perhaps a thick line or your initials would be suitable for this experiment. Press the wax crayon down firmly but not too heavily on the screen. You are trying to fill in the tiny squares between the nylon threads with wax, to block out the ink and thus prevent it from printing. If the crayon leaves pinholes, don't worry. It will not be possible to get the crayon to cover the silk solidly, and the more you try, the more holes you will cause to appear. Later on, when you use lacquer or tusche, instead of crayon, it will be easier. The design you stencil will now appear as the area *without color* on the final print.

A strip of cardboard 1½" wide and 1" shorter than the frame can perform satisfactorily as a squeegee, to pull the colored ink or paint across the screen. Use thick poster or tempera paints; oil paints can be used also, but they are more expensive and not necessary. Water paints are too thin to give proper coverage or pulling consistency. Printer's ink, if you can get it, is best for this experiment.

Before you place the paint dabs on the screen, place a sheet of paper to serve as printing stock under the frame. Use a thick uncoated paper which is not too absorbent. Any color is suitable, as long as it contrasts or harmonizes with the paint.

Place the frame and screen unit over the paper so the screen is touching the paper. Place a paint dab in one of the border areas at the ends of the screen, and add dabs until you have covered the entire width of the screen. With the cardboard squeegee in one hand, pull the paint from the border across the screen, *pressing down firmly* so that the ink goes through the silk on to the printing stock below. Hold the frame steady with your other hand. One stroke is usually sufficient to cover the printing stock com-

pletely; occasionally you may find that you need a second.

Now set your squeegee aside and lift the frame. If the printing stock has stuck to the screen, as it might because of the adhesive quality of the paint, carefully peel it off. You have made a screen print!

Set your print aside to dry while you clean up your work area. (The cardboard equipment cannot be re-used, as it is too fragile to be cleaned, but you may want to keep it as a memento.) When the print has dried—usually only a matter of half an hour or so, depending upon the thickness of the ink deposited on the paper—study it carefully. Notice if there is uniformity of ink on the area supposed to be colored. Examine the layer of paint at both ends of the print. If it is thicker at one end than the other, the pressure of your stroke was uneven, and you should correct this when you print "for real."

Illus. 7. Block out the two ends with masking tape. Spoon some ink on to these areas.

Illus. 8. Pulling the cardboard squeegee across the screen.

Illus. 9. The finished print is not a great masterpiece, but it is valuable for the instruction it can give you. Examine the print closely to see where your squeegee slipped.

Naturally, the equipment you construct for professional prints requires more careful measuring and much sturdier materials than the trial unit you built here. Special inks and screens, of a higher quality than the paint and nylon stocking you used here, are also necessary for fine prints.

The instructions in the following chapters tell the best methods and materials to use for strong equipment and good results. Remember also that your artists' supply shop is the most useful source of information regarding specific brands of inks, solvents and screen fabrics for individual projects.

The purposes of making the sample print are many: you have seen how easy it is to use a piece of fabric to print through, you have made a frame, a stencil and a squeegee (rudimentary, of course) and you have used paint to print a design (primitive though it may be) on paper without much difficulty, and all with your own hands. That is craftsmanship. It is screen printing as a craft that this book is concerned with, and commercial or mechanical practices are not recommended for the true studio screen printer.

3. PRELIMINARY WORK

Now that you are acquainted with the steps in screen printing, start again, this time not to experiment, but for real. Whether you intend to print on paper, fabric, or anything else, the preliminaries of screen printing are always the same. These preparations take up more time than the actual printing process, but investing this time is well worth the effort. This necessary preliminary work may seem like a disadvantage of screen printing, but is a vital part of the entire process. Once you have completed the preliminary work for one series, you can re-use the same equipment for future series. While you are probably eager to make your first prints as soon as possible, take your time now to make sure that your first prints are good ones.

CHOOSING THE WORK PLACE

The best place to work is a room with a lot of daylight, but with windows which you can shade to keep out the direct sunlight. Even more important is a nearby sink with running water. Printing in the open air is not recommended, since even a slight breeze can be annoying. Overheated rooms are just as unsuitable, for if the air is too warm the ink in the screen will dry too quickly—and this can be a nuisance, as it clogs the screen and requires you to clean it frequently. You will need a large firm table to hammer on, and if you can find another smaller table, this will be handy for inks and tools.

MAKING THE FRAME

At this stage you must decide upon the subject and size of the design you will print, because this determines the size of the printing frame. The subject often depends upon the material you are printing on (fabric does not take complicated patterns, for example), but if you are a beginner, start with a subject no bigger than the palm of your hand.

While frames for screen printing can be bought ready to use, as a dedicated printer you will probably want to construct the frame from scratch—both because of the satisfaction you will get, and because of the money you will save. The printing frame is one of the most important pieces of equipment in screen printing, for it holds the screen as tightly as you can make it. The wood strips used for the frame cannot be flimsy or the frame will bend under the tension. The strips or laths cannot be too thick, either, or you will tire your hands when printing.

Spruce, cypress or white pine strips, free from warpage and knots, are good choices for the frame. Buy what are called "double laths" about 1″ thick × 1½″ wide × 6 feet long at a hobby shop or direct from a timber yard or carpenter. The exact dimensions of the laths are not vital here, although very large frames will need thicker sides. If you are a beginner, make a frame that measures 12″ × 18″, to make prints that will be 9″ × 12″. This size is easy to work with.

Keep a supply of laths handy, since you may want to make larger frames later, or other frames the same size as the original for multicolor printing.

While you are buying wood for the frame, also buy strips of wood $\frac{1}{4}'' \times \frac{1}{4}''$, and at least as long as the outside perimeter of the frame you plan to make. At the hobby shop or timber yard, also have $\frac{1}{4}''$-wide grooves cut along the length of the wood laths for the frame, about $\frac{3}{8}''$ from the edge of the laths. After the screen is attached to the frame, you will fit the $\frac{1}{4}''$-strips into these grooves to tighten the screen even more.

Also buy three pieces of $\frac{3}{16}''$-thick plywood, two of them about 3" wide × 11" long, and the third 1" × 11". This wood is for making the squeegee (see page 28).

After buying the wood, you can begin to make the frame. Use a crosscut saw to cut two pieces of wood 16" long, and two pieces 18" long. Saw firmly and squarely so that the wood does not split. You must next fit the four pieces of wood together firmly to make a solid frame.

Mitering the corners as for a picture frame is not suitable here, as mitered corners are not sturdy enough for the tension which the frame will have to bear. Make half lap or tongue-and-groove joints instead. For a half-lap joint, carefully mark the laths with a T-square to prevent a lopsided frame and cut away half the thickness of the lath about 2" from the edge. Attach the laths first with waterproof glue and then with short tacks. If the tacks go through to the other side of

Illus. 10. Marking the wood to be cut for the frame. The width and depth of the cut depend on the thickness of the wood.

15

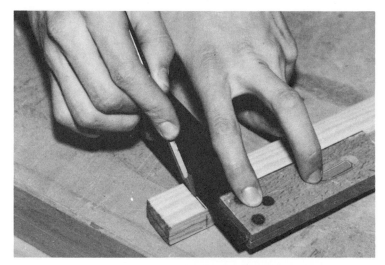

Illus. 11. Professional carpenters and artists use a T-square to guarantee straight edges and square corners.

Illus. 12. Be as careful in cutting the wood as you were in marking it. Cut straight into the lath, halfway through it.

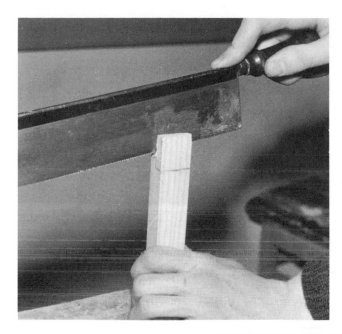

Illus. 13. Then turn and cut each wood lath lengthwise. Use a saw, rather than a knife which might split the wood.

Illus. 14. For extra strength put waterproof glue on both of the laths you are attaching.

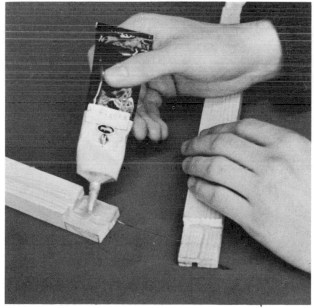

Illus. 15. The half-lap joint holds wood laths together simply, yet securely.

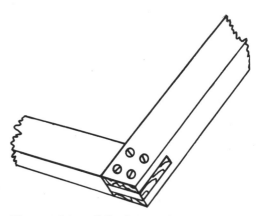

Illus. 16. More difficult to make, yet stronger than the half-lap joint, is the tongue-and-groove joint.

the frame, file or cut the ends off so the frame lies flat.

The tongue-and-groove joint is a little trickier to make, but the sturdy construction that results is well worth the trouble. On one strip, cut away about 2″ of the inside third of the thickness, and on the strip to be attached to the first, cut away one-third of the thickness on each side. Thus, the remaining portion on the end of the second strip will fit snugly into the first. Use both waterproof glue and tacks to attach the strips permanently.

If the frame wobbles a little or is not quite level after the joints have been made and the laths are attached, use a pocket knife to whittle away—bit by bit—any obvious protrusions, and then use coarse sandpaper to smooth the entire frame. The frame *must* lie perfectly flat in order to make uniformly inked prints.

After the glue has dried and the laths are securely nailed together, smooth all rough edges and sides with medium-grain sandpaper. This will prevent the screen from tearing when it is stretched in the frame, and will make you less fearful of splinters while you work.

When the frame is as smooth as you can make it, coat it with shellac or lacquer to keep it this way. This also acts as a sizing, to prevent warpage, and keeps the wood from absorbing paint.

If you have made your frame carefully, it should be quite sturdy and suitable for printing. Frames offered for sale come in any number of styles, from simple wood ones like the one you just constructed, to inflatable frames with air pumps which easily tighten the screen. This home-made frame is fully adequate for your basic needs, and it is both practical and handy: you can lift and move it when printing on large areas (to make the same design on another section of fabric, perhaps), and it is equally suitable for printing on both fabric and paper.

18

Illus. 17. After glueing and nailing the frame together, attach adjustable clamps to the corners and set it aside to dry. The clamps help the glued frame maintain its proper shape.

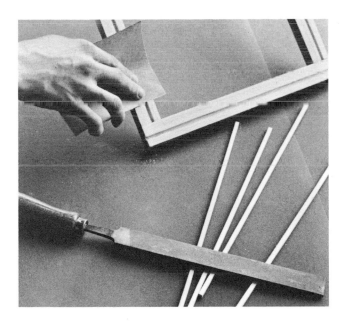

Illus. 18. Smooth the entire frame with sandpaper before you attach the screen. You will insert the thin wood strips shown here into the grooves of the frame after attaching the screen.

If you are printing a large number of separate sheets that are the same size, however, a *hinged frame* is helpful. This is quite easy to make, and needs only the addition of a large, flat piece of plywood or hard fibreboard to the basic frame. See page 26 for instructions for making a hinged frame.

ATTACHING THE SCREEN TO THE FRAME

The material you choose for your screen is the most important factor in the quality of your prints. There are several choices available: Metal wire gauze has a very fine mesh and is good for commercial printing, but it is extremely vulnerable to pressure. Once it is creased, it is impossible to straighten again, and the crease will show on every print. Cotton organdy is inexpensive but it stretches after a number of prints. The threads tend to shift, thus affecting the shape of the stencil. Silk bolting cloth, while more expensive, lasts much longer than organdy and produces sharper and clearer prints. Since a screen made of silk lasts almost indefinitely without stretching or tearing, there is really no point for the serious printer to buy the less expensive yet less durable organdy.

Silk bolting cloth comes in different meshes, ranging from #4 to #20, indicating different numbers of threads to the square

Illus. 19. Fold a hem in the silk and tack it to the frame along the outside border of the lath. Pull as tightly as you can.

inch. The higher numbers indicate a finer mesh, and the finer the mesh is, the cleaner the print will be. You will be able to make prints with very thin lines if you use a fine mesh. The medium-fine #12 mesh silk (126 threads to the square inch) is satisfactory for most general work. A yard of 40"-wide silk is more than enough for a small frame.

Cut out a piece of silk larger than the frame by $1\frac{1}{2}$" on each side. Spread the silk out on top of the grooved side of the frame, and fold a hem on each side of the silk about $\frac{3}{8}$" to $\frac{3}{4}$". Begin to tack the silk to the frame through the hem by pressing thumbtacks or preferably hammering V-shaped brads or carpet tacks in the middle of one of the long sides of the frame, near the *outside* edge of the lath. Place more tacks $\frac{3}{4}$" to $1\frac{1}{2}$" apart along this edge, stretching the silk *tightly* between each tacking.

Now stretch the silk to the opposite long side, making sure that the threads of the fabric are straight, not twisted or pulled diagonally. You will find it easier to work if you sit and hold the frame with the screen side towards you: put the side already tacked on your knee and lean the other side against the edge of the table. This frees both your hands and allows you to put all your strength into pulling the silk up and over the edge of the frame. Use one hand to hold the silk firmly, and the other to press in the tacks before hammering. Silk stands up to a good deal of rough handling, and you should not be afraid of stretching it as tightly as you can. The tighter you make the screen, the sharper your prints will be.

Attach the screen to the two shorter ends of the frame by using the same technique. Again, stretch the screen *tightly* as you fasten it.

You are now ready to tighten the screen even more by inserting those $\frac{1}{4}$"-square

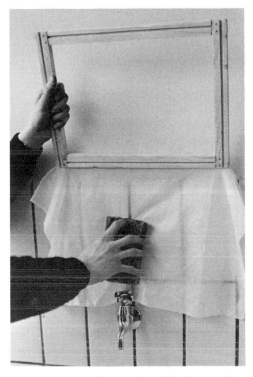

Illus. 20. If you dampen the silk after tacking one side, you will be able to stretch it tauter. The moisture gives elasticity to the cloth.

wood strips you bought into the grooves of the frame. Cut the strips to the proper lengths for the sides of your frame. With the screen-side of the frame facing up, fasten the frame to the table with adjustable clamps, to hold the unit securely while you work. Place the wood strips on top of the silk-covered grooves and carefully tap the strips into the grooves with a hammer. Fasten the strips to the frame with thin nails or tacks. Inserting these strips stretches the screen tighter than you could ever pull it with your hands.

Illus. 21. After you have tacked one side of the screen, tack the opposite side. Begin in the middle and work to each corner.

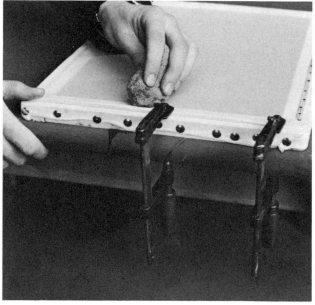

Illus. 22. When all four sides of the screen are fastened, you can still tighten it even more. Insert the $\frac{1}{4}''$-wood strips into the grooves of the frame by hammering them in. Hold them there with adjustable clamps. If you have moistened the screen first, it will not tear.

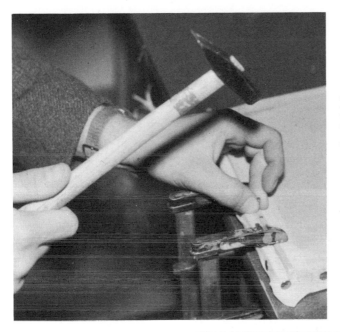

Illus. 23. Hammer nails through the wood strips into the frame. Then remove the adjustable clamps.

Illus. 24. If, after several uses, the screen has lost its original tautness, insert cardboard or wood strips between the screen and the frame. The thickness of the strips depends on how loose the screen has become.

Illus. 25. Cover the edges of the screen with gummed paper strips to prevent ink from leaking through. Cover enough of the screen so there is a large enough space on which to spoon the ink.

Illus. 26. To make sure that the gummed paper strips are completely dry, iron them through clean newsprint with a cool iron.

As you have just discovered, fastening the screen to the frame is not an easy job—it demands strong fingers and, above all, patience. But the trouble you take now will prove very worthwhile, for a screen that is carefully fastened guarantees uniformly colored prints, just as surely as a loose screen guarantees smudged, blotchy ones. Sometimes a screen that has been used for some time and frequently washed loosens and thus makes unclear prints. You can remedy this by cutting wood or cardboard strips $\frac{1}{16}''$ to $\frac{1}{8}''$ thick and about $\frac{3}{8}''$ wide; if these are pushed between the frame and the screen, from the inside of the frame, the screen will regain its original tightness.

Using an adhesive to supplement the tacks is worthwhile, as the screen will then be completely fastened at every point around the perimeter. Waterproof glue is satisfactory for this job.

The screen needs one more preparatory step before it is ready for printing. When you pour the ink on to the screen, you will not want it to soak through the edges. Also, you have to allow space for the squeegee to gather the ink. For your sample print (page 10) you filled up the end borders with tape; here, you need something similar. The easiest way of blocking out the borders is to cover the edges of the screen with ordinary gummed paper strips or thin drafting tape, being sure that wherever two strips meet, they overlap by about $\frac{1}{8}''$. Paste the strips so that one half is glued to the screen and one half to the wood, on either the inside or the outside of the screen. Place newspaper over them and iron with a cool iron to make sure the gummed paper dries thoroughly.

You could also block out the borders by filling in these areas with a water-soluble filler, such as glue, if you plan to use oil-based inks. Use shellac, lacquer, or varnish, for blocking out if you intend to use water-based inks. Apply two or three coats for complete coverage.

It will be helpful at this point to explain just what is meant by the terms "top" and "bottom" of the frame, to make sure there is no confusion later in dealing with stencil-making. The top of the frame is at the same time its inside, that is, the side facing up

Illus. 27. Another way to block out the borders of the screen is to coat them with a liquid block-out material—glue, shellac or lacquer.

Illus. 28. A close-up of a hinged frame. The frame is attached with pushpin hinges to another piece of wood (the printing base), and is raised and lowered as you print new surfaces.

when the printing is done, the side to which the ink is applied. The bottom of the frame is the outside, the part which lies directly on the printing surface when the printing is done, the side to which the screen is attached.

THE HINGED FRAME

To allow the insertion and removal of the printing stock without having to displace the screen with its stencil, it is a good idea to attach the frame with hinges to a printing base. In this way, you can simply raise the screen while you put new printing stock into position and then it will drop into the printing position as before.

The printing base should be slightly larger—perhaps 2″ more on all sides—than the frame. Smooth down the edges and the surface with sandpaper, since any bumps on the base will show up on the print. After attaching the screen to the frame, place the frame screen-side down on the printing base, flush with one side. You will need to use two sets of pushpin hinges to attach the frame to the base. Hinges that are $2\frac{1}{2}$″ or 3″ long are large enough for small frames. Be sure to use pushpin hinges that come apart when the pin is removed. Use $\frac{3}{4}$″-flathead screws to fasten the hinges to the frame, placing the male halves of the hinges on the long side of the frame, and the female halves of those hinges at the corresponding spots on the base. You can then raise and lower the frame like a horizontal door, and it will always fall back into exactly the same place.

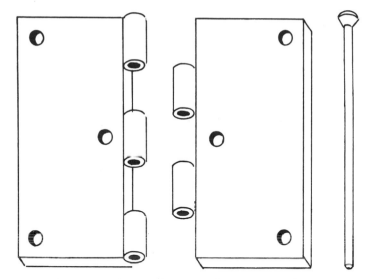

Illus. 29. The female and male parts of a pushpin hinge, and the pin.

By placing the hinges the same distance apart and in the exact same position on many different-sized frames, you can use the same printing base for many frames. Check the screws occasionally to make sure the hinges are not loose. If they are, the frame will wobble and you will not get accurate registration of colors.

Even though hinges are securely fastened, a large screen may sway several fractions of an inch at the opposite end and twist from side to side. To prevent this, nail small wood blocks to the base on each side of the frame at the unattached end. Called cleats, these wood blocks should cradle the frame snugly, so that almost no sway is possible.

You will need one last attachment on the hinged frame: a device to hold up the

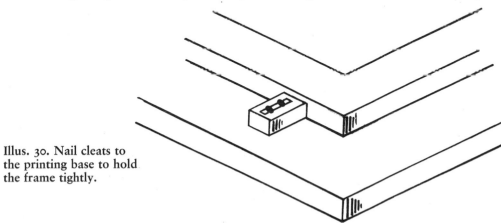

Illus. 30. Nail cleats to the printing base to hold the frame tightly.

27

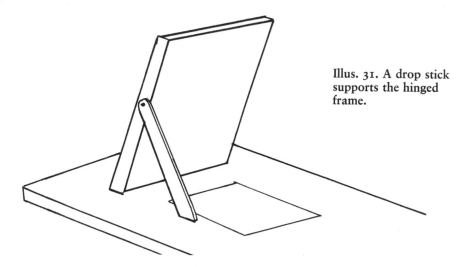

Illus. 31. A drop stick supports the hinged frame.

frame while you are positioning the printing stock on the base. The easiest method is to attach an arm or drop stick to one side of the frame, like those used to prop up the lids on phonographs. You can buy these folding metal supports in a hardware store. Actually, any stick will do.

MAKING THE SQUEEGEE

The squeegee is second in importance in screen printing only to the frame unit. It applies the printing ink to the screen—or, more accurately, it forces the ink through the finely meshed screen on to the stock. Like all the other equipment required for screen printing, squeegees can be bought in many shapes and sizes. The width of the design you are printing determines what size squeegee to use: the squeegee should be at least 1″ wider than the art. If it is too narrow, two strokes will be necessary and a streak will show where the strokes overlap. A store-bought squeegee is expensive, but

making one yourself is quite economical. For the price of one ready-made squeegee you could probably buy the materials to make ten of them.

While you were buying wood to make the frame, you also picked up some plywood for the squeegee (page 15). Two pieces should be 3″ wide and 11″ long, and the third piece should be about 1″ wide and 11″ long. After they have been cut to size, the plywood pieces should, like all the wood you use for your printing equipment, be rubbed smooth with sandpaper.

You will need a rubber strip for the blade. If you can get white rubber, the chances of discoloring the printing inks are less than with black rubber. Polyurethane costs about three times what plain rubber does, but it is worth it—it has the correct amount of spring, wears down slowly, is easy to clean, and is unaffected by most paints and solvents. Polyurethane is manufactured in strips $2″ \times \frac{1}{4}″$ and $2″ \times \frac{3}{8}″$, and is sold by the inch. For squeegees which are longer than 1 foot, use the thicker polyurethane.

Illus. 32. Glue and then nail all the layers of your squeegee together.

The strip should be the same length as the plywood pieces you are using, 11″ in this case. If you are cutting the polyurethane yourself, use a steel ruler and a sharp knife: press the ruler firmly on the strip and draw the knife several times along the edge of the ruler with moderate pressure. If you have access to a paper cutter, this will make a sharper cut. Never use a scissors to cut the polyurethane: the edge will be jagged, and the application of ink on the printing surface will be uneven, resulting in an unattractive print.

Sandwich the narrow piece of plywood between the other two pieces, flush at one side, and insert the polyurethane strip inside this sandwich (see illustration) so that about 1″ of it extends beyond the plywood. Join all the pieces with waterproof glue and short nails or tacks.

When you pull the squeegee across the screen, use a smooth motion. Do not hesitate. Try to scrape the inside of the screen clean of the printing ink you just applied; this motion requires considerable pressure, but promises good prints.

After many uses, the polyurethane blade will wear down, leaving a thicker deposit of ink than you want on the print and a blurry outline of the subject. Sometimes this creates interesting effects, but usually it is not desirable. To sharpen the blade, rub the edge against a sheet of medium emery or garnet paper which is glued to a flat board.

Treat your squeegee with care and it will last for years. Clean it after every use; paint that is allowed to dry on it will eventually corrode the polyurethane. When not using the squeegee, rest it flat on its side, not propped up on the blade end. The squeegee is to the screen printer what the paint brush is to the artist: it is the tool which distributes the color over the printing surface. Uneven distribution produces amateur results, and perfection can be obtained only if you treat your equipment properly.

Illus. 33. When you pull the squeegee across the screen, make one long, straight, continuous motion toward you.

4. MAKING STENCILS

In this section you will learn how to make and use four different kinds of stencils—cut-paper, hand-cut film, liquid block-out, and tusche-glue stencils. There are of course even more types of stencils available for silk screen work, the most notable being the photochemical stencils used in industry and described briefly here. But as these are very difficult to make and require a great deal of technical apparatus, it is better for the home printer to stick to the basic stencils. These are all fairly simple to use and produce enough different effects to satisfy any type of work you attempt.

THE CUT-PAPER STENCIL

This stencil produces a print with sharp, clear lines since, as its name indicates, the stencils are cut from paper. You can make either a positive print, where the design itself appears as color on the printing surface, or a negative print, where the background is color and the design itself is white. Both ways are equally easy with the cut-paper stencil.

Draw the outline of your design directly on the paper you will use as the stencil. Thin paper is best: newsprint (unprinted newspaper) is good, and poster paper is even better. Do not use coated paper, however. An important point to realize is that the thickness of the ink on the printing surface

will be equal to the thickness of the paper stencil plus the screen. The printing surface is distant from the ink in the screen by this amount, so when the ink is forced through the screen, it fills up the thickness. A thick layer of ink, or impasto as it is called, sometimes looks attractive but it takes a long time to dry. For this reason, thin stencils are usually preferable to thick ones.

For cutting the stencil, a professional stencil cutter's knife is worth the investment. It has a thin, narrow blade which makes very fine, detailed cuts. Practice with this

Illus. 34. Lay the cut-out on paper and cover it with the empty screen. The white figure is the silhouette that was cut; the black area is the paper.

Illus. 35. With the paper stencil beneath the screen, spoon an ample amount of ink into the blocked-out border of the screen.

knife until you feel comfortable with it and are proficient at cutting small shapes. A good practice exercise is to cut out the letters of a newspaper headline. To keep the blade sharp, hone it on a fine grain oil stone. Be very careful not to get oil on your hands or on the stencil itself—the stencil will not adhere to the screen if it has grease or oil on it.

When the paper stencil is cut out to your satisfaction, position it on top of a sheet of paper or other printing stock and under the screen. Dab some printing ink across one of the blocked-out edges of the screen, and use your squeegee to spread the ink, thereby making a print. (See page 54, under The Printing Process, for the way to pull the squeegee.) This will make a trial print or proof on the sheet of paper under the stencil, but it probably will not be too good. However, the ink will bind the paper stencil to the screen firmly enough. Before you lift up the first proof sheet, mark its position on the printing base with pencil or strips of masking tape, so you can place a new piece of printing stock as close to the previous position as possible.

You can run off a number of prints, lifting the screen and inserting paper stock for each.

There are obvious advantages to this method of making stencils. Paper is usually available, and is easy to cut. Cleaning the screen of the stencil when you are finished printing is extremely easy: as you wash the screen with water to get rid of the ink, the paper stencil will come off also, and the screen will be ready for another stencil.

Illus. 36. Hold the screen firmly in one hand and pull the squeegee across the screen with the other. Press hard and aim for even, complete coverage.

Illus. 37. When you lift the screen up after pulling your first proof, the paper stencil will adhere to the screen because of the paint. The paper falling from the screen here is the gummed paper which held the printing stock to the printing base (see Illus. 34). Notice the squeegee resting on a can in the background.

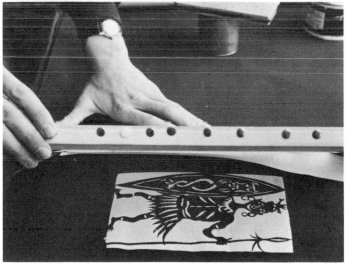

Unfortunately, paper stencils cannot be re-used later; the entire print run must be made at one time. Also, some oil-based paints will be absorbed by the stencil, producing fuzzy lines after only about 50 prints. Still, for the beginning screen printer interested in learning the techniques, the cut-paper stencil is satisfactory.

Illus. 38. If you did not make a complete print, put the screen down again and try to cover the areas you skipped. Before you move the first piece of stock, mark the printing base with pencil or tape to show where the edges of the next paper must lie.

Illus. 39. To clean the screen after using a cut-paper stencil, wash the ink off with water or another solvent. The stencil will fall off when there is no more ink to hold it.

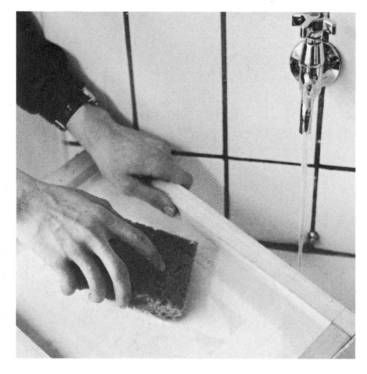

THE HAND-CUT FILM STENCIL

Similar in technique to the cut-paper stencil, the hand-cut film stencil is made of special laminated paper sheets, available at craft shops, from which you cut your design. The sheets have two layers attached together with a temporary adhesive. The first layer is a thin, translucent stencil sheet, and the second layer is a thicker backing sheet made of tissue paper coated with wax. The stencil paper (sold under the brand names of Stenplex in England, and Nu-film or Profilm in the United States) is thin enough to be transparent, so you will be able to see your pencilled design through the paper.

Before you attach the stencil to the screen, you must prepare the screen. For organdy or silk screens, simply sponge with hot water and detergent, rinse with cold water, and set the screen aside to dry. Screens of synthetic fabrics, such as polyester or nylon, must be roughened before they are used for the first time, so the stencil will have fibres to cling to. Sponge the screen with a 10% to 15% solution of caustic soda, *taking care to avoid your eyes*. Rinse the screen first with ordinary white household vinegar and then with cold water. Dry the screen and wash it with a detergent, as you would for a silk screen. After a synthetic screen has been roughened this way once, it later needs only to be sponged with hot water and detergent before you use it again.

Cut a piece of the laminated sheet larger than your design by $1\frac{1}{2}''$ on all sides. Lay this sheet over the design film-side up, and tape it at the edges, to keep it from moving.

Illus. 40. You must prepare screens of synthetic fabrics to accept film stencils or the stencil will not adhere.

35

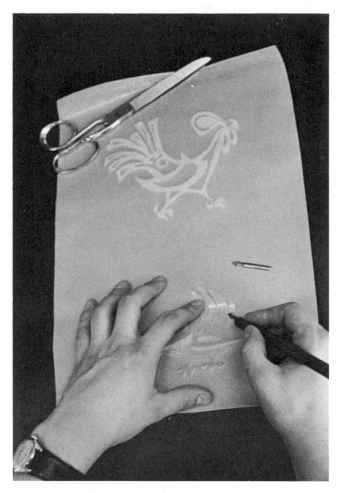

Illus. 41. Be sure your knife is sharp. A dull blade will make you use pressure to cut, but the pressure only presses the two layers together and hinders secure adhesion to the screen.

With a stencil cutting knife, the same one you used for cut-paper stencils, cut around your design *through the top layer only*. Lift off each piece of the top layer as you cut it.

The method of fastening the stencil to the screen (the stencil itself consists of the remainder of the thin upper layer attached to the laminated backing sheet) depends on what type of laminated sheet you are using. These sheets come in different colors,

indicating the different adhesives they contain. Amber sheets are of plasticized shellac, while green and blue sheets use water-soluble glues.

If you are using amber sheets, set your electric iron to the "silk" setting. Place the stencil attached to the backing sheet with the thin upper layer facing up on a sheet of cardboard or an ironing board, and lower the screen until it is in contact with the stencil. Cover the inside of the screen with clean newsprint. Iron with light pressure on the newsprint. Lift the newsprint occasionally until you can see the shellac melting into the mesh of the screen. Let the screen cool. Turn the screen over and carefully peel the backing sheet from the other layer, which is now attached to the screen. Then iron again, without the newsprint, until the stencil adheres completely.

Removing the amber film from the screen after printing is simple. Wash the printing ink completely from the screen (water-based inks can be used, since shellac is not soluble in water). Then flood the screen with alcohol, cover it with a sheet of clean newsprint, and let it soak for 15 minutes. The alcohol dissolves the shellac, so the stencil can be washed off after soaking. Rub the screen with cotton soaked in alcohol to make sure all the shellac is removed.

Blue and green film stencils adhere to the

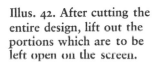
Illus. 42. After cutting the entire design, lift out the portions which are to be left open on the screen.

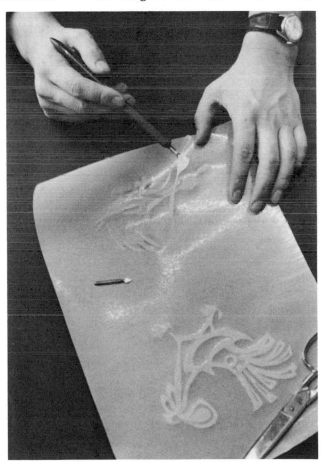

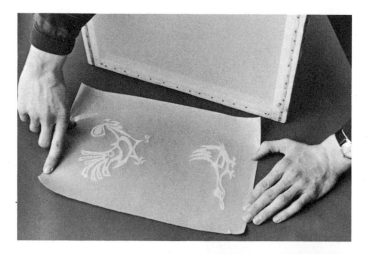

Illus. 43. Place the laminated sheet under the frame, making sure that it is positioned exactly. If there are any very large areas where the film has been removed, cut a small slit through the backing sheet. The slit allows air to escape.

Illus. 44. Iron first through newsprint and then directly on the amber sheets. If working with green or blue sheets, use a combination of moisture and heat, or the manufacturer's special solvent.

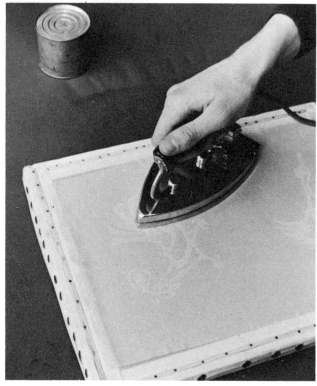

Illus. 45. When the film is cool and dry, turn the screen over and slowly peel the backing paper off. If the film starts to come up with the backing paper, turn the screen over again and re-apply the film.

screen with water, because their glue is soluble in water. (However, these stencils therefore cannot be used with water-based inks.) To attach the blue stencil to the screen, dip a rag in cold water and squeeze it as dry as you can. Place the screen over the stencil and rub the inside of the screen briskly with the damp rag, thus slightly moistening the stencil film. Lay a sheet of clean newsprint on the inside of the screen, and iron this quickly and lightly. The moisture and heat will melt the glue so it sticks to the screen. Remove the laminated backing sheet the same way as for an amber sheet.

To fasten green stencils, put the green film, thin upper layer up, on the table and lower the screen on top of the film. Place heavy weights on each corner of the frame to hold it down firmly. Set up an electric fan or hair dryer to blow across the screen, and dip a rag into a mixture of alcohol and water. Wring the rag as dry as you can, and rub the inside of the screen with it. Do not go over the same place twice with the rag. When the screen turns a strong green, the glue has penetrated the mesh. Leave the fan or hair dryer blowing until the glue has dried, and peel off the backing.

Both blue and green films are removed in the same way: clean the screen of ink with mineral spirits (paint thinner) or a solvent suitable to the ink you use. Mop the screen dry, and then hose the inside of the screen with hot water. Peel the stencil off, and sponge the screen with hot water and detergent to get rid of any remaining glue. Rinse with cold water and dry.

SCREEN PRINTING

Illus. 46. When cutting letters or sharp corners, allow each cut to extend slightly beyond the design. The extra length of the cut will melt when you attach the film to the screen, and the film will be solid.

You can create unusual effects with film stencils by specially treating the stencil before you attach it to the screen. Use a wood burning tool to melt the edges of the stencil rather than a knife to cut it. The fuzzy edges which result will print blurry outlines, which resemble lithographs or charcoal drawings.

Save the scraps of film that you cut from the backing sheet. If you mix some film solvent with these scraps in a jar, you can use the solution to touch up weak spots in a stencil, or even to block out new areas on your screen with a brush. Once the film solution is painted on the screen and the solvent has evaporated, this stencil can be printed and then removed just like the stencils you cut and ironed to the screen.

THE LIQUID BLOCK-OUT STENCIL

The liquid block-out stencil, sometimes called the lacquer stencil, is probably the oldest method of making stencils in silk screen printing. The production could not be simpler: basically, you paint the part of the screen that is *not* to print with lacquer, shellac or glue, so that the liquid fills in the holes of the mesh screen and the ink cannot pass through. A fine mesh screen is important for sharp outlines, although you may sometimes prefer the soft edge obtained by using a looser mesh. When the ink appropriate to your particular block-out liquid is applied to the screen (water-based paints cannot be used with water-soluble glues, for example), the color goes through

40

the uncoated sections of the screen to the printing stock below.

Before you start working, cover the worktable and the floor around you with old newspapers. This advice may sound fussy, but it is a sound recommendation: lacquer stencils are often quite messy. Assemble all your materials on one end of the table. Draw the design to be printed (called the "art") on light-colored paper with India ink or another dark ink, so that its outlines clearly appear through the screen. Make the art small enough so there is a clear strip at least 2″ wide on each end of the screen for an "ink-carrying area," to get the squeegee moving easily. The 2″-strip must be coated with gummed paper so ink will not penetrate the screen in these places (see page 25).

Place the frame with its bottom or screen-side down, so that it rests on top of the art.

Outline the art on the screen with a sharp, medium-soft pencil to indicate the areas that are to be covered by the lacquer. Then remove the art, but keep it handy in case you want to compare it with the screen. Turn the frame over so the bottom of the screen is on top. Because the liquid you will use may drip through the screen, put a layer of newspaper on the base.

You are now ready to start applying the lacquer, shellac or glue. The liquid should not be so thin that it runs when you apply it to the screen; if it is too runny, leave it in a shallow bowl for a few minutes until some liquid evaporates. Start applying the lacquer with a flat bristle brush on the large open areas, but make the first coat a thin one so the lacquer does not immediately penetrate the screen. While this first coat is drying, use a pointed sable brush to coat the small

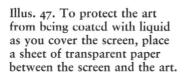

Illus. 47. To protect the art from being coated with liquid as you cover the screen, place a sheet of transparent paper between the screen and the art.

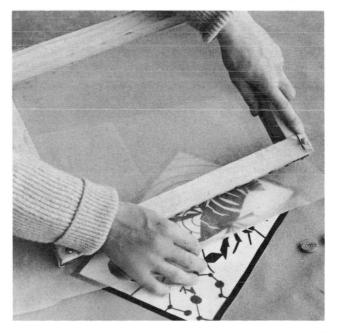

spaces around the lines of the art. If your hand needs support while you are painting, lay a lath or flat board across the frame to rest your hand on.

Turn the frame over occasionally so you can catch any drops of lacquer that are hanging and paint them flat. After coating the frame thoroughly, leave it alone for about an hour to dry. Hold the frame up to a spotlight to make sure that no part has become porous during the drying; occasionally pinholes develop, and these will make small dots on the print. If there are holes, paint over them with more lacquer. For special effects, you may want more pinholes: after the glue has dried, dampen a rag in the appropriate solvent and quickly run it over the screen. Some glue will be removed, leaving holes.

If you should slip and paint some lacquer in the wrong area, immediately try to wash it out with solvent. Once the stencil has dried it is almost impossible to remove lacquer from the screen. Use lacquer thinner,

for lacquer stencils; alcohol, for shellac stencils; and water, for glue stencils. Wash that portion of the screen clean of any special remover so the ink you use is not affected by it.

The outside edges of the screen also need to be coated with lacquer, so that no ink can ooze between the screen and the frame during printing. Use your wide brush, and cover the places where the frame and screen meet to make sure it is impermeable.

While making a lacquer stencil is simple enough, it does take a lot of time and patience to outline a design accurately. The details of the drawing on the screen are limited because of the viscosity of the lacquer. Lacquer stencils are still very practical for the beginner, since the stencil is rugged and stands up to all kinds of silk screen inks without additional reinforcing materials. These stencils are also just about the least expensive kind to use for silk screen printing.

Illus. 48. Use a pointed brush to block out the narrow areas close to the design.

Illus. 49. For added coverage, coat the sides of the screen with the block-out medium.

THE TUSCHE-GLUE STENCIL

Tusche is a marvelous liquid used in lithography and only recently applied to silk screen printing. It is a waxy substance which does not dissolve in water, but does dissolve in paint thinner, turpentine or kerosene. You paint the design—the area that is to appear in color—on the screen with tusche, and then cover the entire screen with glue. When you dissolve the tusche with a solvent, the glue covering the tusche no longer has anything to cling to, and the design area is thus clean and free of any material. Oil-based inks must be used with the tusche-glue type of stencil, since water dissolves glue.

Set the screen on top of your original art

Illus. 50. Pour some tusche from the bottle into a bowl and let it thicken slightly. Then apply it thickly to the screen.

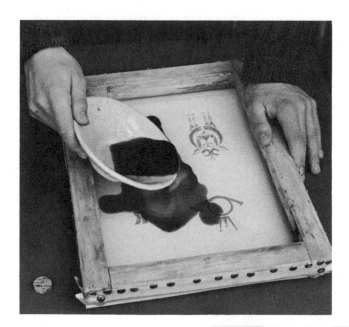

Illus. 51. Pour the tusche solvent on the screen, making sure it gets into all corners. Let it soak the tusche for about 15 minutes.

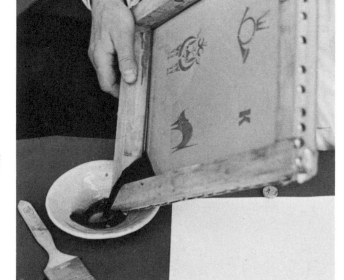

Illus. 52. If you poured a lot of solvent on the screen, pour the excess off before you begin to rub the screen.

and fill in the proper areas of the screen with liquid tusche. Tusche is dark and feels waxy, but it is the consistency of paint and can easily be brushed on the screen. To opaque an area completely, apply the tusche thickly; in some cases, it may be necessary to apply two coats, but let the undercoat dry first. Set the screen aside until the tusche is as dry as possible. Tusche rarely dries completely, but remains slightly sticky. When it reaches this state, you are ready to apply the glue.

Ordinary glue is perfectly suitable for the tusche-glue stencil. Just be sure it is *water*-soluble and that it will not dissolve in paint thinner or kerosene. You may need to thin the glue; add small amounts of water until it can be easily spread.

Pour a little of the glue-water mixture on the taped border of the screen, not on the open screen. Use a piece of cardboard or matboard as a squeegee, or use a wide brush, and spread the glue over the entire surface of the screen. Let the glue dry, and

Illus. 53. Hold the screen up to a light to check for pinholes.

then hold the screen up to a spotlight to check for pinholes. It is not unusual to have to give the entire screen a second coat of glue.

After the glue has dried completely and you have filled in all the pinholes, you must dissolve the tusche with kerosene or thinner. Put a number of sheets of newsprint under the screen and pour the thinner over it. Leave the screen alone for a while (about 15 minutes) and then use a cloth to rub the areas where you painted the screen with tusche. The tusche will run into the newsprint; remove the top sheets occasionally

for a new absorbent surface. Rub both sides of the screen until both the tusche and the glue which you applied over it have dissolved and no more black from the tusche appears on the newspaper.

If some spots of tusche cling to the screen, try rubbing the areas carefully with a small stiff brush. If the tusche does not dissolve at all in a certain area, it might be due to a thick layer of glue at that spot. Dab a few drops of water on the glue at the difficult places, to thin it slightly. Then apply more thinner and proceed in the usual way.

Dry the screen by rubbing both sides with

Illus. 54. Lithographic crayons and pencils, used as tusche is used, come in several degrees of hardness. Use the harder ones for fine detail in your stencils.

Illus. 55. Do not shift the screen or fabric as you draw, or the pattern will be lost.

a cloth. Make sure that all the glue is attached where you do not want ink to print, and that the tusche has been dissolved. Then the tusche-glue stencil is ready to print.

Besides liquid tusche, another material, lithographic crayon or pencil, made of a harder wax than liquid tusche, can also be used. Rub the crayon on the screen just as if you were drawing with an ordinary wax crayon as you did in your sample project. Make litho crayon stencils the same way as tusche stencils. With litho crayons, you can achieve a great variety of effects by drawing over textured fabrics such as burlap, net, or even over wire screen. An unusual and interesting porous design will appear on the print. Turn the page for examples.

Illus. 56. Some patterns which result when you rub lithographic crayon over textured materials.

THE PHOTOCHEMICAL STENCIL

For professional serigraphy, photochemical stencils definitely produce the best results. Subtle shadings and half-tones can be produced by this method, but the equipment required is generally too elaborate and expensive for at-home printers. The following is only a brief description of the process. If you are curious to attempt the photochemical method of stencil-making, there are several excellent books available which deal with photochemical stencils in detail.

The screen itself is coated with a special photographic emulsion. The best kind is one that is easy to use and gives sharp prints without distortion of the pattern. The store where you buy your supplies will be able to help you choose the best brand of coating. This coating material comes in two bottles: one contains the emulsion itself, and the other contains the substance which makes this emulsion sensitive to light. Mix the liquids in the proportion of 10 to 1 in a dark bottle. Coat the entire screen uniformly with this liquid and leave it lying flat in a dark, warm room to dry.

If you want to print a picture that contains gradations of color, the image will have to be "dot screened"—that is, photographed on to a film which translates the light and dark shades into areas containing few or many dots. When viewed at a distance, the dots combine to look like solid areas. (Look closely at a picture in a newspaper to see the dots of a coarse screen.) The negative of this dot-screened picture is printed on to another film, making a halftone positive, which is used to make the stencil for the print. While in the negative the light and dark areas appear opposite to what they really are, in the positive the light areas are actually the light areas of the picture itself.

There are thin plastic foils which you can cut to create an original design, rather than reproducing a photograph; these are cut and then placed directly on the silk screen itself. By using these foils, you eliminate the photographic processes of enlarging, reducing and developing the film, but you will not be able to produce any halftone shadings.

Place the positive film or foil over the silk screen, which you have already coated with the light-sensitive emulsion, and expose the entire screen to light for a certain length of time. This time is usually determined by experimenting to see what length is best for your particular equipment. The areas on the screen which are exposed to the light harden after a time, but those portions which have been covered by the dark areas of the film remain soft. Flood the screen with warm water after exposure, until all the soft emulsion is washed away, and chill with cold water. Leave the screen to dry for about an hour, and proceed with the printing as usual.

Illus. 57. To prepare the screen for a photo-chemical stencil, first coat it with photographic emulsion.

5. SILK SCREEN INKS AND AIDS

Special tacky inks are needed for silk screen printing, just as in every other printing technique. The distinctive feature of silk screen inks is their consistency: the inks must have body. The colors are therefore in an emulsion about the consistency of poster paint or thick cream which prevents the ink from flowing too loosely on the screen, but at the same time makes it easy for the ink to be applied evenly to the screen. Silk screen inks also must not dry too quickly on the screen, as they would clog the mesh; yet they should dry more quickly than letterpress inks, so that after only a short drying time the printed matter can be stacked. Finally, while silk screen inks should adhere well to the screen, you must be able to remove them by simply washing the screen with the appropriate solvent.

The base of the ink you are using, either water or oil and synthetic resins, is one of the factors which determines your choice of stencil: the ink and stencil must be opposite in nature, or neutral to each other. Water-based inks, for example, cannot be used with a block-out stencil of glue, since glue dissolves in water. Yet amber film stencils cannot be loosened with water, so water-based inks are used with these stencils. The neutral shellac stencil is good for all types of inks, since shellac dissolves only with shellac thinner.

Beginners should not be scared away by the large assortment of stencils and inks. The easiest and most inexpensive silk screen ink to use with just about any stencil is a water-based ink. The great advantage of this type of ink is that you can thin it with water if necessary and after printing simply wash it out of the screen. It prints on paper, wood and cardboard, and is suitable for all work that does not have to be weather-proof—indoor posters, advertising, pictures. Water-based inks come in strongly opaque colors, which can be mixed together to provide an even wider range of shades.

Besides water-based inks, a number of other special inks can be bought for all kinds of printing stocks. There are specialized inks for wood, glass, vinyl, hardboard and sheet metal, which make a scratchproof and weather-resistant surface. Even foam rubber can be given an elastic and hard-wearing color.

Textile inks, which are of particular interest to us here, have a good reputation, and rightly so: the progress that has been made in developing them to their present excellence challenged chemists for many years, but the inks we have now are worth their efforts. The oil-based inks used for textiles must be much more durable than, for example, an ink that is to be printed only on paper, since the screened fabric will be worn and washed. In addition to the general requirements for all silk screen inks, textile inks must adhere firmly even if only a very thin layer of ink is applied. Also, they must not only be washable but must sometimes tolerate boiling temperatures. They should be sunfast, that is, not fade in light. Finally, and most important, the inks must remain flexible on the fabric, so that printed cloths of fine quality will retain their flowing, graceful character.

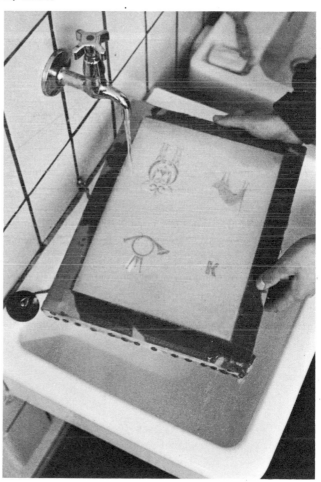

Illus. 58. Remove water-based inks from the screen by flooding the screen with warm water.

Illus. 59. To remove stubborn patches of ink that have begun to dry in the screen, create a more forceful jet of water by placing your finger over the faucet.

The silk screen inks for textiles that can be bought today satisfy even the most demanding printers. The inks come in a wide variety of colors and, like inks for paper, can be mixed to obtain even more shades, even though they are transparent. When applied, the ink, being transparent, provides light shades, and by adding an extender you will print even more delicate veils of color. By overlapping these colors, you create new and surprising shades and effects, greenish blues and lavenders, for example. If you add white to the ink, however, it will become so opaque that you can print even black materials with bright colors. The ordinary "vat dyes" used by the textile industry are not suitable for silk screening; because of their chemical composition, these dyes often need complicated treatments, such as developing their color in acid vapors after they are printed. Silk screen printing inks are much easier to use, although they sometimes must be dried with heat for permanence. But do pay particular attention to the following advice when using textile inks:

Never let the ink dry in the screen. Print briskly, and not in an overheated room. Clean the stencil immediately after the last print has been made. If the screen becomes clogged with dried ink, it can be cleaned only with a fine bristle brush and xylene, a chemical solvent. Take care to see that no ink gets on your clothes. Ink spots on a white shirt will unfortunately demonstrate only too well how durable the ink is. Always wear an artist's smock or apron while you work.

As you gain more experience, you will experiment and use a variety of special inks—dull, glossy, transparent, opaque, weatherproof. These finishes are usually best when you use an oil-based paint, but be sure you have the correct thinner and cleaning preparation for any water-insoluble inks. Also, special "screen cleaners" are available for the treatment of screens clogged with dried ink.

To prevent small prints, such as cards and signs, from sticking to the screen after squeegeeing, thereby causing unclear prints, buy an adhesive which can be sprayed on the base in small quantities before printing. It makes papers, cards and even small pieces of fabric stick to the base, rather than the screen, and does not leave any residue on the paper or fabric. After printing, you can easily peel the printing stock from the base.

Illus. 60. Mix a sufficient amount of ink on a glass sheet before you pull your first proof.

6. THE PRINTING PROCESS

Whether you are printing on paper, fabric or a more unusual material, the actual process of applying the ink to the printing surface in silk screen printing is almost the same in every case. The general remarks here are applicable for all screen printing; additional advice for printing on special surfaces is included later.

While the preliminary work for screen printing is rather lengthy, the printing itself takes very little time. Though it is simple, it demands a lot of concentration and quite often an ability to make quick decisions. Make it a habit to have all the tools and materials you will need on hand before you begin printing, so that everything goes smoothly and without hesitation.

You have already made your preparations in a well-lighted room, and you have one large and one small table. If there is enough space in the room, place the big table near the source of light, and be sure that you can walk around it. This is a particularly good arrangement when large sizes or lengths of fabric are to be printed. (In printing large areas, work with a companion. One of you can raise and lower the frame, while the other removes and replaces the printing stock. You should be able to print small areas by yourself.) To protect the floor from being spattered with ink, and to keep the printing surface free from dust, cover the floor around the table with old newspapers.

On the table itself, lay clean, plain newsprint several layers thick, and put the base of the screen on top of it.

FURTHER PREPARATIONS

Prepare as much of the printing stock as you will need—the size of the sheets you buy or cut depends of course on the size of your subject. Absorbent or rough-edged hand-made paper is particularly suitable. For your first trials, have plenty of cheap paper—absorbent duplicating paper or unprinted newsprint—upon which you can pull proofs and make trial runs.

In addition to the printing frame, there should be a large can on the table, on which you will rest the squeegee when you are not using it. On the smaller table, have a shallow bowl containing a small, moistened natural sponge. You will need this whenever part of the screen clogs during printing, which might happen if the ink is too thick or the room too warm.

All the inks you will use or might need, including black, white, and a thinner or extender, should be on the small table. Also, have several small screw-top jars, a glass sheet with a palette knife, an old spoon, and a few rags. Nearby, keep adhesive tape, scissors, a thin bristle brush, thumbtacks and ordinary pins. Their uses will be explained.

MIXING THE INKS

First mix the inks in very small trial quantities on the sheet of glass. With the palette knife, take a little of the lighter colored ink, and add the darker shades to it gradually, so you get to know the way the different colors combine with one another. The appearance of a color on glass is not always the color that will appear on paper, however. To make sure your mixture is a good color, brush a small sample of ink on the paper that is to be printed, and leave the sheet to dry. If your sample dries to a satisfactory color, mix a larger quantity of ink in the same proportions as the sample in one of the screw-top jars. Add a few drops of water or thinner to the mixture if necessary, until it has the right consistency—like thick cream. If the ink is too runny, the print will be blotchy and "bubbly." If the ink is too thick, the meshes of the screen are liable to clog. Should you accidentally make the ink too thin, pour the contents of the bottle into a shallow bowl or saucer and stir it near a source of heat, until part of the emulsion evaporates and the ink is a little thicker. Then use the spoon to put the ink back into the screw-top jar.

MONOCHROME (ONE-COLOR) PRINTING

For the first proof printing, lay a large sheet of clean uncreased newsprint on the printing base and place the frame on it, with the side to which the screen is attached (the bottom) face down. Then either spoon or pour directly from the screw-top jar a ridge of ink about $\frac{1}{2}''$ to $\frac{3}{4}''$ thick on one of the blocked-out ends of the screen, either the top or the bottom. Apply some ink to the rubber edge of the squeegee with a spatula, so that the edge will glide more smoothly.

Now you are ready to make the first stroke with the squeegee. You must hold the frame firmly against the base while you run the squeegee quickly over the whole screen. Use slight pressure downward as you pull the squeegee towards you. As the screen must be completely covered with ink right from the start, immediately run the squeegee over the screen again in the reverse direction, unless you feel that the first application may have been made too thickly. Put the squeegee back on the can.

While you hold the edge of the printed paper to prevent it from sticking to the

Illus. 61. Spoon ink on to the ink-carrying area. The upper portion of the screen will be used for a second color.

screen, carefully raise the frame a little without changing its position to see from the side that all parts of the paper are uniformly printed. If they are not, lower the screen and apply the squeegee a third time. Occasionally, though rarely, you may need to do it four times. If the first proof printing is not a brilliant success, do not be discouraged—it rarely is. As you gain experience, your prints will improve.

The squeegee should be kept at a constant pressure and speed as it pulls the ink; do not slow down as you reach the end. If you do not use enough downward pressure, the ink will flood under the screen, producing an unclear print. After a few prints, you should be able to judge exactly how to manipulate your equipment.

If you are satisfied with the first proof, start printing the planned quantity at once. The most efficient way to work is with an assistant. You raise the screen while your assistant removes the completed print and puts it aside to dry. While he is hanging it from a clothespin, putting it in a professional drying rack, or even placing it on the floor, if there is room, you put the next sheet on the printing base. Make sure that the corners of the second sheet are in exactly the same position that the corners of the first one were. This "registration" is not so important when printing in one color, but it is vital when using more than one, so that the different colors overlap or meet each other at exactly the right places.

Exact registration for monochrome print-

Illus. 62. Before you remove the first proof, place register marks around the edges of the stock and the screen. Then every color will be printed in the same position on the paper as on the first print.

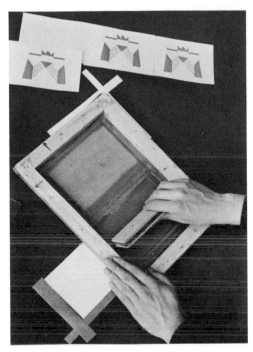

Illus. 63. Hold the frame with one hand and pull the squeegee with the other. Notice the prints drying above the frame.

ing is best produced by placing register guides on the printing base. The guides can be pencil marks, tape or, for most accurate placement, small blocks of wood. If you use pencil marks to indicate the corners of the printing stock, take care each time you position a new piece of paper that it falls exactly into the proper place. Pieces of tape are easier to see and they can even be "felt" as you lay the paper down, but for the most accurate registration, use wood blocks. Nail a block to the base at one end of the sheet of paper and one on each side. The paper will fall in between the blocks and

require no adjustment. Registration for polychrome printing is a bit more complicated and is described in that section (page 58).

After a few prints have been made, you and your assistant will have established a routine and rhythm. If you do not alter this pattern, the printing should go smoothly. However, if you hesitate, slow down your pace, or stop to admire your prints, the ink in the screen will clog. You will then have to wash the ink off, repair the stencil, and take a new proof. To avoid these bothersome tasks, work as quickly—and carefully—as you can.

CLEANING THE SCREEN

After you are finished printing a series (as the group of prints made from one stencil is called), you should clean both the ink and the stencil from the screen so you can re-use the screen later for another design. Clean the screen *away* from the printing table; it can be a messy job and the printing table should be reserved for printing only.

First, remove the excess ink from the screen with a spatula or cardboard scraper and put it into the jar in which it was mixed. Label the jar and store it to use another time. If you have used a water-based ink, rinse the screen thoroughly with a jet of cold water, and then wash it in warm water with a little detergent. Rinse again with cold water and set the screen aside to dry.

For an oil-based ink, flood the screen with paint remover or a special solvent purchased from your ink supplier. Let the screen soak in this solvent for 10 minutes. With a rag or a piece of cardboard remove as much ink as you can; then take a clean rag soaked in solvent and rub the screen. Wash it in warm water and detergent, scrubbing with a bristle brush if necessary. Rinse with warm water until the screen is clean.

The procedure for removing the stencil from the screen is included in the section explaining stencils (see page 31). Follow the special instructions that come with a particular stencil if you are using an unusual material.

POLYCHROME (MULTICOLOR) PRINTING

Whether you are working on paper, fabric or anything else, you are probably anxious to start printing in several colors. But you should not try multicolor printing until you are fairly successful with printing in one color. Multicolor printing requires additional preparations.

Each separate color requires a separate stencil. If you have several screen and frame units, you can make all the stencils at the same time and thus reprint later if you want. If you have only one unit, as is usually the case, you must make one stencil and print one color at a time.

On your original art, indicate with colored pencils which areas are to be in which color. Then place the screen over the art and proceed to make the appropriate stencil for your first color. (Always print the lightest color first.) When you print this color, mark the corners of the printing stock on the base with register guides so that you can replace the stock *exactly* in the same place when you print subsequent colors. Make the number of prints you will want, plus several additional ones (their use is explained later). Then remove the stencil and ink from the screen.

Place the cleaned screen over your original

art and prepare the stencil for the second color. When you print the second color on the sheets, position them exactly, following the register guides. To pull a proof with the second color, coat the screen with ink and print on one of the extra sheets from the first run. (Use one of your poorer prints.) This is called a "makeready" sheet, and you will probably discard it. You may have to readjust the color or consistency of the ink, but the frame will be properly positioned over the sheet, thanks to the register guides. The fact that you made the second stencil by following

Illus. 64. If your frame is not hinged, the frame is not fastened to the base and you must register the frame as well as the paper. Outline the second color sections on tracing paper and place the screen over this. Following the tracing paper, prepare the stencil.

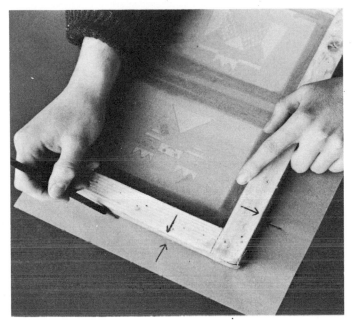

Illus. 65. After making the stencil, mark both the frame and the tracing paper so you will be able to replace the screen in the proper position. The tracing paper is necessary because it allows greater accuracy in positioning the frame unit.

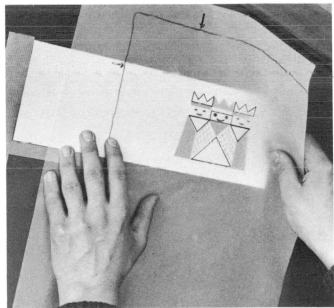

Illus. 66. Remove the screen and slide your first print (with one color) under the tracing paper. Place register guides around the printing stock.

Illus. 67. Place the frame over the tracing paper by lining the parts up according to the marks you made. Slide the paper away and make register guides for the frame. Both stock and frame can now be removed or raised, and then replaced correctly.

the same art as the first ensures that the stencil is in the right position on the screen, and your register guides guarantee that the screen and frame are correctly placed over the paper. Once everything is set up correctly, the second color is as easy to apply as the first.

Continue making stencils and printing until you have printed the different colors of your art. For variation, try overlapping some colors to create new shades and tones. You should experiment with different colors and varieties of inks on your printing stock before you print the series anyway, to be sure that your ink gives total coverage to your surface. Try different kinds of inks and different combinations of colors to see which give the most pleasing results.

7. PRINTING ON UNUSUAL SURFACES

Screen printing is usually done on flat (not embossed) paper or cardboard, and paper surfaces present very few problems to the printer. The absorbent paper is receptive to almost any type of ink, the ink dries rapidly, and once it is dry, the ink is permanently fixed to the paper. Other surfaces, however, do not accept the ink so readily and require special treatment to keep the ink from peeling off. Glass, metal, plastic and wood are the materials to which the screen printer usually has difficulty adhering the ink. The smooth, non-porous surface, which looks tempting to decorate, proves deceptive: the ink glides on the slippery finish with ease, but it peels off just as easily unless certain preventive steps are taken.

All grease and oil must first be removed from the surface. For most metals, commercial vinegar is a satisfactory cleaning agent which dissolves the grease but none of the metal. For wood, use turpentine to remove any protective lacquer coating. Alcohol is the best cleaning substance for glass. For plastics, however, the specific plastic you are printing on will determine the exact solvent, as well as the specific ink, you should use. Consult the seller or manufacturer of the plastic to determine what is best, and always test small patches of the plastic yourself with various cleaning products before you begin printing. Because plastics vary from glassy lucite to rubbery vinyl, no one substance can be used for all. Your ink and solvent supplier is the best source of information for anything regarding the adhesion of the ink to the printing surface.

Once you have thoroughly cleaned the material of all grease, you must choose the proper ink for this surface. To decide on both brand, category and color of ink, make a small smear of several inks on the cleaned surface. Allow at least 24 hours after printing before you evaluate the suitability of an ink for a particular surface. While the drying time of the ink is usually less than an hour, the extra time permits you to check adhesion of the ink to the surface.

To achieve permanent adhesion on metals, it is sometimes necessary to add a small amount of thinner to the ink. The thinner will in no way affect the screen or the drying time of the ink; it simply brings the ink into closer contact with the metal. Again, your crafts supplier is the best source of information for these materials.

Printing on cloth is performed with basically the same procedure as for paper, and requires only a few special materials. Because it is so popular, the details of textile printing are given here in an entire chapter.

8. PRINTING ON CLOTH

While most aspects of printing on cloth are the same as on paper, there are several specific requirements that you should consider. The question of subject is of course most important. On paper, practically anything can be printed, but you are somewhat more limited in your choice for textiles. Elaborate outlines that resemble tapestries, landscapes that require three-dimensional effects, and very detailed still lifes are almost impossible to print on textiles. This is because the pattern of the weave of the material conflicts with the screened pattern of the stencilled picture itself, giving a confusion to the printed design on the fabric. Too much detail in the picture would only make a messy, confused print.

A pattern used several times on a length

Illus. 68. Print your design on paper several times, then cut these prints apart. Arrange them on your cloth in various positions to find an attractive repeat design. Page 67 shows the result of this experiment.

Illus. 69. A repeat design on cloth makes an attractive border for curtains. This pattern was printed in bright peacock blue on sand-colored silk.

of fabric (or wallpaper) is called a "repeat." A repeat design can be effective, even if the single design is uninteresting, because the unprinted parts—the white or pastel areas—have a decorative effect themselves if the subject has been cleverly placed. Thus, the material will show both an "intentional" pattern, based on the printed design, and an "unintentional" pattern, made by the un colored sections. To test the effect of the repeat, first print the subject a few times on paper or outline the shape on colored paper. Then cut out the prints or shapes and place them in various ways on the material. (For these tests, print with ink for paper and wash the stencils immediately after, so they can dry for the cloth printing.) Pin the paper cut-outs to your fabric so you can place the stencil directly over it when you print. It is not

always easy to decide on the best arrangement of the pattern from among the many possibilities. Finding a good repeat requires taste and practice.

This is just as true in the choice of colors. If you are a beginner, start printing on cloth in one color, and add the second color only after you are practiced with the first. Too many colors confuse the repeat, so do not add a third or fourth color until you have acquired some experience and skill. Good silk screen inks, except white and black, are transparent, and charming combinations made by overlapping are possible with them. Color samples, mixed well on a glass palette and then applied to a small strip of the fabric, will prove to you that on a thick material such as linen, even light colors will "take," while a finer fabric—silk, for example—needs an application of brighter, deeper colors. Remember that a very fine material can absorb only a thin coat of ink, so the color must be a vibrant one if it is to show when applied thinly.

CHOOSING THE FABRIC

You should be able to print successfully on almost any kind of fabric. Just be sure that your design and the weave of the cloth harmonize with each other. Bold subjects are well suited to coarse fabrics, while finely detailed designs would show up best on smooth, thin materials.

The advice is often given to beginners to make their first textile prints on plain, inexpensive material such as unbleached calico or muslin. While these fabrics are quite printable, most subjects lose force and expression on the unbleached and rather rough material. The background will detract too much from the design. Instead, buy a length of low-priced white or light-colored cotton or synthetic fabric, meant to imitate silk. These fabrics are quite attractive when they are printed, and while they might not be too durable, they can make colorful curtains, scarves, dresses, place mats, or innumerable other items.

For a curtain or cover for a cushion, select a material with some body to it. There are various linen materials, both natural and man-made, which offer a wide selection. Because of the particularly beautiful texture of these fabrics, extremely large patterns are just as effective on them as small subjects. For dresses, blouses, tablecloths and napkins, you will want a fabric with a more flowing character. Try cotton or another soft material.

Illus. 70. The indigo motif covers the entire area of this scarf of silver-gray silk.

Pure silk is undoubtedly the finest and most expensive material for silk screen prints, so do not attempt to print on it until you have some experience and feel fairly sure of yourself. "Silk" means only pure, natural silk. Although artificial silk (such as nylon and other synthetics) is technically suitable for printing, it lacks a softness which fits this technique so well. Also, synthetic silk may crumple easily when worn or used in other ways. If you have to make a choice, use a fine cotton fabric rather than artificial silk. However, you should be able to find surprisingly inexpensive remnants of silk in

Illus. 71. Curtain material that has been screen printed with a pattern of lines, then accented by large solid areas of printed color.

small quantities, if you watch the stores carefully.

There are three kinds of silk that are particularly interesting for screen printing:

1. *Pongee* silk has a medium to close weave. Because of its dainty, filmy character, pongee is particularly suitable for printing ladies' scarves and handkerchiefs.

2. *Foulard* is an attractive, closely woven fabric with a slightly diagonal texture. It can be used for men's and ladies' scarves as well as for lightweight blouses.

3. *Tussore* or natural silk (*Honan* and *Shantung*) has a charmingly irregular texture. It is a wonderful material for dresses and blouses. The more densely woven grades of tussore silk are excellent for distinctive neckties.

PREPARING THE FABRIC FOR PRINTING

Almost every kind of material has been refined in some way; usually, it is passed through a starch solution, stretched, and calendered. The addition of starch, called the dressing or finish of the fabric, makes it fuller and gives it body. However, when the fibres are covered with the starch, the fabric can absorb only a limited amount of the silk screen inks. When a heavily dressed material is printed, the colors may flake off after a time, or even vanish completely when the fabric is washed or boiled. You must therefore remove the dressing before you print, so that the fibres can accept as much ink as possible.

Screen printing on textiles requires special inks, but the process is
the same as that for paper. Cut-out paper stencils were moved
across the fabric to make the repeat design here.

66

A repeat design demands careful preplanning to prevent a too-busy pattern.

For any material but natural silk, first rinse in cold water. Then wash briefly with a detergent made for fine fabrics, and rinse clean again. Next, add about a tablespoon of malt extract to a bucket of rinsing water, stir until the malt has completely dissolved, and soak the material in the malt solution overnight. The malt converts the starch into sugar, which you can then easily wash out of the fabric. Finally, rinse the material, let it dry, and iron it.

Merely boiling a new material once does not guarantee that all the dressing has been completely removed. Soaking in a malt solution is therefore recommended for linen, cotton and man-made fibres. As a rule, natural silk has only a light dressing or none at all. Wash silk with a fine detergent, then rinse it and, before it dries, iron it smooth on the back of the material.

You may not always want to print on a white material. White of course soils very easily, and it makes every color printed on it look harsher than it would on a tinted background. A colored material frequently looks more becoming, even before anything has been printed on it. You can tint and dye any white material with dyes which are inexpensively purchased. As a rule, a light tinting of the material will be enough, for colored subjects appear to their best advantage on pastel shades. Follow the instructions carefully. Dyeing involves no risk, even if you are completely inexperienced. But to be on the safe side, experiment with a small piece of the material first, to make sure the color is not too dark and that no annoying stripes will appear on the fabric. If you add a little vinegar to the last rinse, the color will be brighter and will have a pleasing gloss when it is ironed.

After completing any necessary preparations, cut a short strip from the material on which to test the printing ink, and roll up the large piece in plain newsprint, to prevent creases and protect it from dust until you are ready to use it.

FASTENING AND PRINTING THE FABRIC

There is one more important difference between printing on paper and printing on fabric: fabric must be stretched and then pinned with ordinary straight pins to the printing base. Use the large table itself as the base, and cover it first with an ironing cloth and then with plain, clean newsprint. Stretch the material over these layers and fasten it with straight pins, heads pointing out and close together. Mix enough ink in small screw-top jars, and have your frame, squeegee, sponge and other equipment ready.

Take a proof on a piece of extra fabric (perhaps at the end of the length) to test the color and consistency of the ink and to cover the screen with ink. Then move the frame itself to the desired position and arrange the stencil exactly over your paper pattern. Lift the frame slightly so you can remove the paper; then lower it again and print. Move the frame to the next area where the design is to be, and print. It is helpful to have an assistant to remove the paper pattern.

If you prefer not to use paper patterns, or if the repeat design is such that you can regularly lift the frame and replace it on the fabric a few feet away, you can mark the sides of your table to show you where to place the frame. First lay the fabric out evenly on the table and pin it to the newsprint underneath. Either draw guide marks along the side of the table or use tacks, nails or additional hinges to which you can fasten the frame. As you print, you lift and reattach the frame as you move down the fabric.

Illus. 72. Portion of a curtain. The pattern is steel blue and the background is beige. The stencil used for this printed fabric was a hand-cut film stencil (see page 31).

69

Light flowers on a bright
background make a lively
decoration. Exact color
registration is not vital in a
helter-skelter design such as this.

An abstract bird stands out against a background of deeper colors.
Transparent inks create new shades when they overlap.

Delicate flowers as well as bold splashes of solid shades are
possible in screen printing. Use a brush to swirl liquid stencil
on your screen.

When you finish printing the length of fabric which is pinned to the table, remove the frame and set it aside. Unpin the fabric and slide it off the end of the table, keeping it unfolded and uncreased. Let the area you just printed lie over and between a few chairs while it dries, and pin the next area to be printed to the table. Print this new area as you did the first surface, and then, if there is still more cloth to be printed, move the fabric down again.

TREATMENT OF FABRIC AFTER PRINTING

Immediately after the last printing, wash out the stencil. Then examine the cloth to discover any places where imperfect impressions were made. Correct these with a brush and ink as much as possible, before the printed ink has dried completely. On linen and the coarser fabrics, the corrected spot will hardly be visible; on silk, however, it will be obvious. Silk prints, therefore, should never be corrected or improved after printing.

Lift the material from the base and attach it with a few pins to the wall or floor, where it should be left undisturbed to dry for at least 24 hours. When dry, cover the printed parts of the material with clean, plain newsprint and iron with a moderately hot iron. The heat will evaporate the last residues of emulsion, making the material more resistant to washing and boiling. Large printed lengths can simply be passed through a hot ironing machine after the printed side has been covered with newsprint to protect the roller of the machine. Do not wash freshly printed materials until at least a week after printing; the ink needs about six days to harden sufficiently on the fibres.

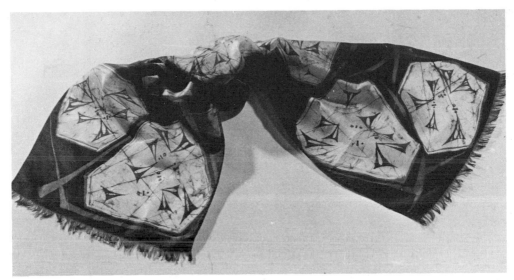

Illus. 73. This scarf was first screen printed and then batiked in a warm dye bath. The unusual yet attractive patterns which result in batik cannot be predicted by the craftsman.

9. SCREEN PRINTING COMBINED WITH BATIK

Screen printing and batik are fundamentally two different techniques. While both make materials colorful and decorative, each process does so in a very distinctive manner. In screen printing, the ink is applied to the surface of the fibres and is closely bonded to them, while in batik, a dyeing process, the fibres are impregnated by the ink. It is not difficult to distinguish two pieces of cloth decorated by these different methods: screen prints have well-defined areas of color, while the different areas in batik designs usually fuse together softly. Of course, neither technique is strictly limited to these effects; it is quite possible to make a silk screen stencil that produces cloudy, indistinct areas of color, or a batik design with sharp outlines which make the design look as if it

An Oriental motif in vibrant red and blue is surrounded by the dark border of the printing stock.

Four versions of fruits represent the four seasons of the year. This series of pictures appears on the top of a calendar.

A free design like this is best stencilled by lightly drawing on the screen with a brush dipped in a liquid block-out material.

had been printed. But generally, the two methods of decorating fabrics are quite different, and even an inexperienced craftsman will easily recognize the two types.

In spite of the differences in character, batik and silk screen can be used together on the same material. You may be surprised by the interesting effects the combination produces. A large solid area of soft color, which is usually produced when batik is used, sometimes needs a stronger subject with clearly defined lines to enliven it. Conversely, a screen print with a few clearly outlined shapes might be enhanced by the softness of new colors generally applied over the surface. The two methods of decoration have rarely been used together, perhaps due to the lack of knowledge by one craftsman about the other craft. With the invention of new aids for each craft, there is no longer any reason to limit yourself to only one decorative process.

CHARACTERISTICS OF BATIK

Batik is not a printing process but a method of dyeing. Hot wax is decoratively applied with a brush or a cup with a spout (called a *tjanting*, purchasable in a craft shop) to thin, light-colored cloth. After the wax layer has hardened, the entire cloth is dampened and then put into a vat of warm dye. Only the parts not covered by wax will absorb the dye. When the material has been rinsed clean and dried, the wax is either removed or left on, and additional areas are covered with wax. Then the material is immersed in a second dye bath. This procedure can be repeated several times, depending on the desired design.

During the dyeing, the cooled layers of wax usually break and crack in various ways.

You can encourage these cracks to appear by crushing the waxed cloth. At these cracks and fractures, the dye penetrates into the cloth, making the "crackle" designs that are typical of batik. This characteristic of the wax guarantees the spontaneous character by which you should be able to recognize batik. It is rarely possible to know in advance what the final batik pattern will be like. The cracks in the wax, the fusion of the different dyes, and the varying depths of color produce a unique, novel charm in each work.

Batik requires quick judgment. The more unhesitatingly and surely you apply the patterns with the wax brush, the more unusual and striking will be their effect. Fussy and intricate designs look painfully labored.

The advantages of batik when used in combination with screen printing are many. Empty-looking spaces between the printed parts can be tinted different colors. Even large batiked areas seldom give monotonous effects, thanks to the varied crackle designs and the gradations of color. An unsuccessful printing on expensive silk material can be "rescued" by a batik treatment: the faults will be hidden by new and different arrangements of colors.

Not all textiles, however, are equally suitable for batik. The experienced artist in this technique usually restricts himself to pongee and foulard silk, and he may also use a thin, wax-permeable cotton fabric. Heavy linens and cottons are out of the question for batik work. While in silk screen printing very long pieces of material can be printed without difficulty, in batik the size of the fabric is limited. The piece of material must not be too large to be immersed easily in the dye bath. The dye bath must have a fairly low temperature, below the melting point of the wax, which itself is low. Batik-

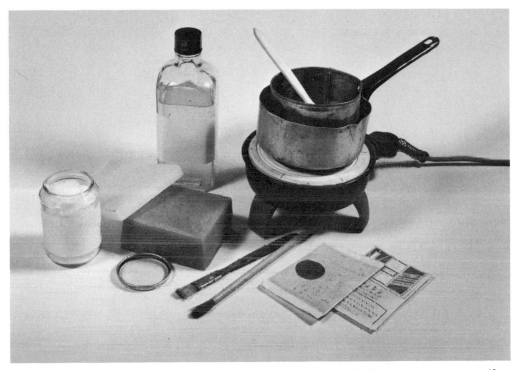

Illus. 74. Here are some of the basic materials necessary for batik, listed clockwise: paraffin, beeswax, dry-cleaning solvent, an electric hot plate on which stands a metal can in a pot, dyes, and paint brushes.

treated materials should therefore only be gently washed, and they must never be boiled. Batiked silk is generally cleaned in dry-cleaning fluid.

THE BATIK PROCESS

You will need the following materials: a spirit lamp (one which burns alcohol) or electric hot plate (or, if nothing else is available, a thick candle), a metal can in which you will heat the wax, either paraffin or beeswax, a variety of inexpensive brushes

with synthetic bristles (animal hair bristles may burn in the hot wax), a tjanting, straight pins, dyes, a large plastic or enamel bowl, tongs or rubber gloves, an electric iron and ironing board, plain newsprint, waxed paper, and dry-cleaning solvent.

Lay several layers of newsprint on your worktable and cover the newsprint with a sheet of waxed paper. Then place the cloth, either screen printed or plain, on top of the waxed paper and pin it in place along the sides. The newsprint insulates the work surface and keeps the wax from cooling too

Black and white penguins parade across a rose background. A tusche or litho crayon stencil creates the rough, uneven edges which contribute to the casual artistic effect.

A complex print such as this scene, requiring many stencils and many different printings, demands talent, knowledge, accuracy, imagination, and above all, patience. Choose your printing inks carefully, as they are what determine the quality of your finished print.

quickly, while the waxed paper keeps the batik from sticking to the newsprint when the cloth is waxed. The cloth will instead stick to the waxed paper, which you can later easily peel from the fabric.

Cut the paraffin in small pieces and melt them in the metal can over the hot plate or candle until they are completely liquid. You can also melt them by placing the can in a bath of boiling water, so the aroma of the melting wax is not too pungent. If you use an electric hot plate, place an asbestos sheet under the can. This prevents the wax from spurting out on to the heating element, as it might do if there is too much heat. The smell of burning wax is most unpleasant. Adding a little beeswax to the paraffin makes

it more elastic and easy to work with, but this is not absolutely necessary.

With a paint brush or your tjanting, deposit hot wax on the cloth in various designs and swirl patterns. If you have screen printed the cloth, cover the printed areas with wax also, to prevent them from being colored again. You can also try your hand at creating representational designs, but be forewarned: painting with wax is very tricky, and your lines will probably not be perfectly even. The imperfections which almost always result appear more attractive when they are part of an abstract pattern than if they are supposed to represent something accurately.

After you have waxed the design, let the wax cool and harden. Turn the fabric over

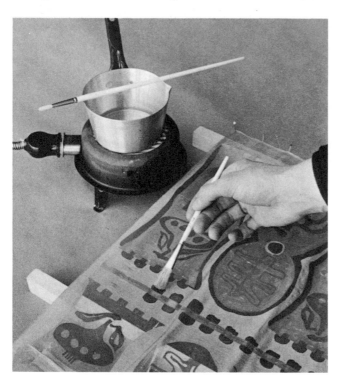

Illus. 75. When you paint wax on the cloth, you might want to raise the cloth from the table with wood laths. The wax can then penetrate the cloth more thoroughly.

Illus. 76. When using a commercial tjanting, place the unmelted wax in the reservoir. As you heat the wax, it will run out the spout. Guide it above the cloth to create finely designed patterns.

(the waxed paper will be attached to it, since the wax you applied to the fabric will have penetrated and bound the waxed paper) and peel the waxed paper off. Do not peel the *fabric* from the *paper*, as the waxed areas will crack when you bend them. Examine the wrong side of the fabric closely to make sure that the wax has penetrated the cloth. If areas need touching up, dab some wax on them.

The cloth is now ready for its first dye bath. Almost any dye meant for fabric is suitable; there are several brands which need very little preparation. Prepare the dye according to the directions on the package and, if it was prepared with hot water, allow it to cool until it is lukewarm. (A dye bath which is too hot will melt the wax on the cloth.) Unless the dye package advises you differently, add one tablespoon of un-iodized salt for each gallon of liquid dye, or one teaspoon per quart, to help the dye adhere to the fabric.

Wet the cloth before you immerse it in the

dye bath. When the cloth is in the dye bath, it will look much darker than it will when it dries. Leave the cloth in the bath for the amount of time that the package directs and then remove it with a pair of tongs or rubber gloves. (Some dyes contain chemicals which may be harsh on your hands.) Do not squeeze or wring the cloth, or the wax will crack. Hang the cloth to dry, but save the dye until you see the finished color. You may want to re-wet and re-dye the fabric to obtain a darker color.

When the cloth is dry, it is ready for the second waxing. In this waxing, which will be followed by a second dye bath, cover some of the areas you just dyed, to keep them the color of the first dye bath. Give the cloth a second dye bath in another color exactly as you gave it the first dye bath, remembering that the dye must be lukewarm and that the cloth will look much darker when it is wet. There are no exact instructions for the second waxing, but generally it is best not to introduce new patterns with the wax drawings. Rather, fill in the empty spaces generously and imaginatively with shapes similar to those already batiked. A pointed brush or tjanting is particularly useful for making the designed "handwriting" free and unrestrained. These free lines suit the

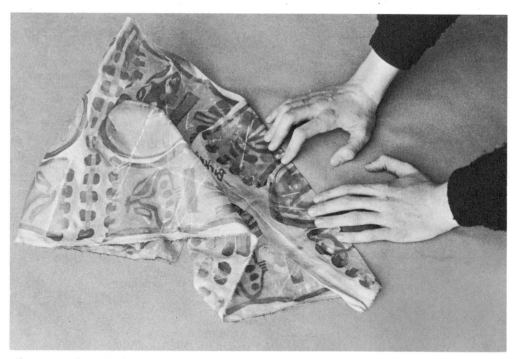

Illus. 77. Before the last dye bath, bend and fold the waxed cloth in a few random places. The hard wax on the fabric surface will break, causing the dye to penetrate to the cloth for the famous "crackle" effect.

Illus. 78. Since the bowl containing the dyeing liquid is probably not too big, the cloth you dye cannot be too large either. Use a stick or wooden spoon to stir the cloth gently.

Illus. 79. When the cloth has been in the dye bath long enough (remember that the color looks darker when wet), remove it and rinse it with lukewarm water. Keep rinsing until the water runs clear, but do not squeeze or wring the cloth.

Illus. 80. To remove the wax from the cloth, place newsprint over the fabric and iron both thicknesses. Remove the newsprint when it becomes saturated and replace it with a new layer. Iron until no more wax goes into the newsprint. Then use dry-cleaning solvent for the remaining wax.

essential character of the batiked design very well. Make the second dye bath darker and stronger than the first, and the dyeing time longer. Rinse the cloth in lukewarm water until the water runs clear.

After the second dyeing, there will be three shades on your cloth: the original color of the cloth, preserved on the sections you covered with wax before the first dye bath; the color of the first dye bath, in the areas you covered during the second waxing; and the shade which results as a combination of the two dye baths, on those areas which you left completely unwaxed. You can continue to wax and re-dye as many times as you wish, but take into consideration the harmony of colors and amount of detail you want on the cloth. If you are planning to combine batik with screen printing, do not make the batik design too intricate.

REMOVING THE WAX

Allow the cloth to dry completely before you remove the wax. Removing the wax while the dye is still wet will cause the dye to bleed (that is, run) into the undyed areas, creating blurry lines and indistinct areas of color.

Place many layers of newsprint on your ironing board, cover with the batiked cloth, and then cover the cloth with more newsprint. Set the electric iron at one setting *lower* than that appropriate for the fabric, and iron through all layers with even pressure. The wax will melt from the heat of the iron and be absorbed by the newsprint. Remove the layer of newsprint both immediately above and below the cloth every few minutes so that there is a new surface to absorb the wax.

When the newsprint no longer absorbs any wax from the cloth, stop ironing. There will still be a dark area around the places where the wax was, since the iron cannot remove all of the wax. To remove these dark spots, you must clean the batik in solvent or dry-cleaning fluid (follow the directions on the package carefully and work in a well-ventilated room), or take the cloth to a dry cleaner.

To avoid the necessity of working with solvent, you might coat the entire cloth with wax, if the area is not too large. When you remove the wax by ironing, the whole piece of fabric will be darker, due to the slight amount of wax left clinging to the fibres. There will be no difference among the separate areas, though, and thus no reason to remove all the wax completely with solvent.

When the batik is free of all wax, or is uniformly covered with the least amount possible, lay a cloth soaked in white vinegar over the batik and iron it, to set the dye and smooth out any wrinkles. Your batiked cloth is now ready to be mounted, sewn, or screen printed, if you did not do so before.

Illus. 81. "Lakeside with Reeds." This print was made with white ink on a black background.

10. POSSIBILITIES FOR SCREEN PRINTING

Let's say you have made your frame with painstaking care, sanding and shellacking the wood strips and forming rigid, square joints. You have purchased the finest silk screen available and have attached it to the frame as tightly as can be. Your stencil is perfect, there are no pinholes, and you have bought the inks which are suitable to the stencil. Your squeegee is a work of expert carpentry; all its edges are square, the polyurethane edge is sharp. You print quickly yet carefully, and your prints show how expert you are. But now after you have done all these things and are pleased with the results—what are you going to do with your prints?

Illus. 82. Preparing a stencil with lithographic crayon for a small run of posters. The artist keeps the original art close by so he can compare the stencil to it.

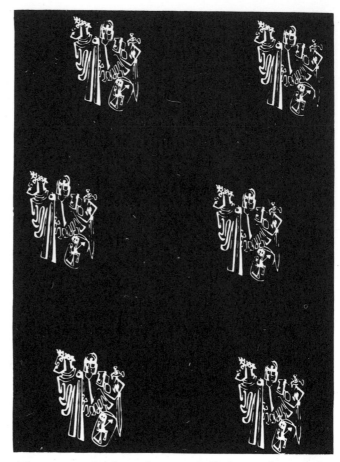

Illus. 83. The abstract motif above, which seems to have been inspired by Roman statesmen, is randomly repeated on the background to the right. Wallpaper, wrapping paper, curtains and other large areas do well with a repeat design.

Suppose you printed on paper. There are as many possible uses for screen prints on paper as there are for paper itself. The most logical idea, of course, is to frame your print and hang it on the wall. Sell the rest of the prints in the series, or present them as gifts. Their value is always realized, and many famous artists now work in the screen printing medium. You may be one of them. If you are more modest, however, or your prints are small, use them as covers for personal greeting cards. Or decorate the borders of many small sheets of paper, for stationery. If you print on thin paper in large sheets, you can use your results as decorative wrapping paper. For a small run of posters, perhaps to advertise a one-time-only event in a small town or on a university campus, screen printing gives professional results without professional cost. The covers for the programs for the event can also be screen printed. To make your prints last for years, you might laminate them in plastic: place your print between two sheets of clear,

Illus. 84. The original art, left, was copied on to the screen and printed with white ink on a dark background to produce a regiment of moustached and feather-capped soldiers. A single design can take on new meaning when used as part of a repeat.

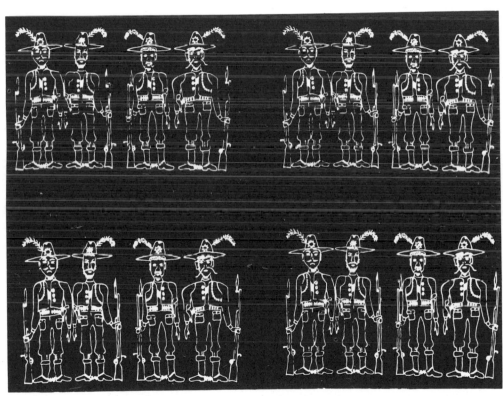

sturdy vinyl and place a dry cloth over the layers. Iron lightly with a cool iron. The heat of the iron will melt the plastic just enough to stick the two sheets together permanently, your art sealed in-between. You can use the plastic-sealed art as place mats if you want.

Printing on textiles is, after paper, the most popular surface for printing. Screen printed cloth can be used wherever you use any other cloth. Clothing is probably your first thought. If you have used the proper inks, you can wear your printed fabric without any fear of the colors fading or washing out. Ties and scarves are popular items to decorate also. Use a large piece of fabric as a wall hanging for an unusual decoration or, if you can stand to do any-

thing but admire your work, put the cloth to a more practical use. Tablecloths, bed-spreads and curtains are articles that are usually overlooked, probably because of their customary sameness. Call attention to these home accessories by designing and printing colorful fabrics for them.

Did you ever think of decorating a shower curtain? Vinyl is a plastic and requires special inks, but decorating a shower curtain is certainly no more difficult than decorating a cloth tablecloth or a poster. You can print on plastic to make a tablecloth, or design a shower cap to match the curtain.

If you have any ability in carpentry (and if you made your own frame, you probably do), you can make your own signs out of wood and then screen print the proper

Illus. 85. A non-repeating pattern can still be a symmetrical one. The nativity scene here by Wiltraud Jaspers was prepared from a simple block-out stencil, painted on the screen with a narrow brush.

90

Illus. 86. There are two simple methods of making a shaded background. Apply a liquid block-out over the entire screen, and remove some of the substance by rubbing with a sponge moistened in solvent. Then apply the solid figures of the stencil. Or, rub litho crayon on the screen over a textured material (see page 47); then apply the rest of the stencil.

Illus. 87. This design, used on a poster, was screen printed from a photochemical stencil for clear, straight lines and fine detail. A hand-cut film stencil could also have been used.

Illus. 88. The rooster and duck motif, shown on the back cover and again on page 67, was screen printed on a fine silk to make an attractive scarf.

message on them. Or make several small boxes and, instead of painting them, print on them. Old dressers and sideboards will look new again if you decorate their drawers with colorful printing. Coasters and trays are easy to print on: their small surface requires only a small stencil. Remember to remove any old varnish and paint before you print, so that your designs will adhere properly to the wood surface without peeling after several years.

Any place that looks empty can probably be enlivened in some way by screen printing, no matter if the place is a wall, fabric or furniture. Look around you; open your eyes; use your imagination. You are sure to discover new and interesting surfaces to decorate.

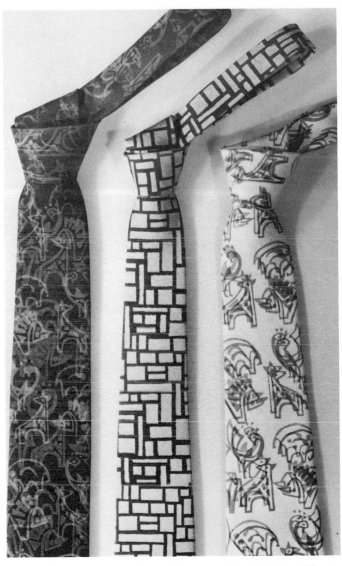

Illus. 89. Handmade neckties of screen printed fabric. The tie in the middle has an unusual mosaic-like pattern, while the other two—which used the same stencil—were printed with a repeat design purposely out of register, to form an original eyecatching design.

INDEX